# SOCIAL INJUSTICE IN KHALED HOSSEINI'S NOVELS

## A STUDY THROUGH THE KITE RUNNER AND A THOUSAND SPLENDID SUNS

**MR. ABHIJITH. K. B & MR. D. PRADEEK**

Copyright © Mr. Abhijith. K. B & Mr. D. Pradeek
All Rights Reserved.

To God Almighty

# Contents

# CHAPTER ONE

# INTRODUCTION

Literature is a reflection of cultural and social life. It reflects the environment in which it is produced. Literature is one aspect of the cultural edifice, which has its roots in the social, political, economic, philosophic, and religious patterns of time. Literature, in fact, gives vent to those multidimensional conscious and unconscious issues of a society which seek gratification and realization in the real world.It is a component of the larger cultural complex from which it emerged. Because their writings affect and help shape public image, writers have a social obligation. Readers judge the social aim, intellectual depth, and emotional honesty of their writings consciously or unconsciously. Violence is frequently depicted in literature. In many ways, literature from the twentieth and twenty-first centuries reflects pervasive violence, from ultimate annihilation through nuclear warfare to individual crimes of rape, murder, and abuse. Both the spectacular attraction of violent activity and its capacity to shock and upset readers by disturbing their beliefs have received adequate treatment from critics.Following World Wars, writers expressed concerns about living in a world that looked incapable of long-term peace and in which human hostility threatened to wipe out the human species and civilization entirely. As a result, numerous writers from the modern to contemporary eras have sought to depict the historical, psychological, and creative landscape of a modern world riddled with and torn by violence.

Like the literature of other countries, Afghan literature hailed from regional languages like Pashto, Dari, Tajik and Turkic. The medieval period of Afghan literature was written in these languages. The royal courts of regional empires such as the Samanids, the Ghaznavids and the Timurids supported the writers. Other regional and linguistic groups had rich oral traditions but occupied a minor place on the national literary scene.

The roots of Afghan English literature can be traced back to the subcontinent where the ancient art of story-telling continues to flourish in Afghanistan, partly in response to widespread illiteracy. Centuries-old tradition of presenting folktales through music and spoken word has evolved into a highly developed and well-liked art form. In Afghan society, folklore has become the thread that connects the past with the present. Folktales are often used to teach traditional values, beliefs in Afghanistan. The seventeenth century Afghan warrior-poet Khushal Khatak (1613- 1694), who wrote in Pashtu, is regarded today largely as the national poet of modern Afghanistan. His popular theme of the noble tribesman later became popular with other writers also. His contribution to the growth and development of Afghan literature is highly significant.

Many of the literary elites fled to exile after the Russian invasion in 1979, where they coupled guerilla activity with reappraisals of the principles they formerly championed. Khalili, Abdua Ghafur Arezo (Director of the Iranian Cultural Association), Kazim E Kzimi, Fazl Allah Godsi, and Sami Hamed were among the writers in refugee camps. Wasef Bakhtari, Ghahhar Asi, Parto Naderi HaideryWoojudi, and Azam Rahnavard Zaryab were among those who remained in Afghanistan. These authors, as well as those who had left abroad, focused on the hardships of exile. Atiq Rahimi, whose work Earth and Ashes, first published in Dari in 2000, became a bestseller and was adapted into a film directed by the author himself, may have been the most successful author in exile.

Mahmud Tarzi was probably the first contemporary Afghan writer and journalist to publish satirical works. Later, defying the censors, Haj Ismailn Harati and Shayaq Jamal promoted satirical poetry. Several poets, such Talib Qandihari, Nazir Nasib, and Shirali Qanum, have bravely attempted to mirror the difficulties of Afghanis' daily lives and the peculiarities of their social interactions in their satiric works in recent years. Due of the oppressive and ever-present censorship, their satiric works were limited to price gouging, superstition, and low-level governmental corruption. Satirical sketches and cartoons provided a new dimension to the Afghan satirical repertoire about the same time.

A burgeoning group of leftist writers gathered around Noor Mohammed Taraki (1917-1979), a journalist, novelist and short story writer who was influenced by Theodore Dreiser, John Steinbeck and Upton Sinclair. Suleiman Layeq (b 1930) and Bareq Shafiyee (1931) are poets in both Dari and Pashtu exemplify the development of these activities. Initially they wrote religious poems, but after 1953, when the Shah of Iron was installed, Afghan poets were much influenced by the leftist literature produced underground or in exile by writers of the outlawed pro- Soviet Tudeh party. This new wave of Afghan writing was heavily imbued with European socialist and existentialist forms, and the ideas of Jean- Pal Sartre and Albert Camus were blended with Sufism. Mahmud Farani (1930), Mahmud Rahim Elham (1931-2003) and Saaduddin Shpoon (b 1933) have equal facility in both Dari and Pashtu, in prose and poetry. Zia Qarizada (1922 -2008) made major contributions with the poems in Ashur-i-nau (New Verse, 1957), written in Dari. The woman writer Kubra Mazhari (1950), Dari poet, novelist, and short story writer, edited the literary magazine Erfan in the 1970s.

A distinguished group of prose writers have written history and philosophy in the Dari language. Ahmad Ali Khzad (1915-1983) Afghanistan's first archaeologist wrote Afghanistan darShahnama (Afghanistan in the Shahnama 1976). Qassim Rishtya (1915-1998) wrote Afghanistan darNazdahquran (Afghanistan in the nineteenth century, 1958). Leading socialist historian Mir Ghulam Mohammad Ghobar (1899-1978) wrote Afghanistan dar Maser-i-tarikh

(Afghanistan's path through history, 1968). Hasan Kakar (1932) wrote Government and Society in Afghanistan (1979) in English. Abdul Hai Habibi (1908-1984) historian of Pashtu Literature and Bahauddin Marjooh (1928- 1987) and Ghulam Ghaus Schodjaie are essayists in social philosophy.

Since the early twentieth century, one of the most significant cultural breakthroughs in Afghanistan has been the translation of foreign fictional texts. With the establishment of the printing press in the country, modern translation paved the door for greater cultural transformations. Its evolution tracks the country's socio-political shifts. At its inception, translation was used to introduce a new way of life (the Western way of life) as part of a political campaign to improve Afghan society. One of the main goals of such a project was to modernize Persian by making it more simple and representative of ordinary life.Sofar, translation of foreign fiction was perceived to be one of the main sources for the emergence and 6 development of modern fiction and its various genres, such as novel, short story and drama. The field of short story writing includes Hassan Kaseem (1994), Ghulam Ghaus Schodjaie (1940-1979), Sharifa Sharif (b 1953) and Spozhmai Zaryab (1949). Their works dealt realistically with every day contradictions inherent in a society in the process of modernization.

Since 2001 the focus of writing has been on newspaper and magazine production and publishing poems focusing on experience of the past twenty years. New publications in the style of the epic stories and in the great literary tradition of the past are rare, and writers find difficult to publish prose on subjects other than current social issues and politics. The most successful novels since 2001, The Kite Runner (2003) and A Thousand Splendid Suns (2007) by Khaled Hosseini, were written by an Afghan who immigrated to the United States at the age of fifteen. While these books have raised an interest in Afghanistan beyond the current war among readers worldwide, they have been controversial among resident Afghans.

Khaled Hosseini is currently one of the most widely read author in the world. He shares the stories of his Afghan countrymen and women, highlighting their suffering, sorrow, and challenges that make their life a living nightmare. He is a man on a mission, a quest to rid his country of all its faults and restore it to its former glory. He accomplishes this by producing beautiful novels with gorgeous scenery that are widely distributed throughout Afghanistan and around the world. It covers the tale of the Afghan people, including Afghan women, children, and men, who are entangled in a web of religion, politics, and terrorism. So far, he's published four books: 'The Kite Runner', 'A Thousand Splendid Suns', 'And The Mountains Echoed' and 'Sea Prayer'. His works have been sold in over eighty countries and have sold over 45 million copies. His first novel, The Kite Runner, was adapted into a huge film and named a Book of the Decade by The Times, Daily Telegraph, and Guardian. Richard & Judy named A Thousand Splendid Suns the Best Read of the Year in 2008.

The Kite Runner was released in 2003 and received a lot of positive reviews. Hosseini's youth in Kabul inspired some of the works. Amir, an Afghan man residing in San Francisco, is the protagonist of The Kite Runner. He gets a call from Rahim Khan, an old friend of his fatherwho lives in Pakistan, and it reminds him of his youth in Kabul, Afghanistan. Amir recalls his beautiful youth in Kabul, where his father was a successful businessman. Amir lives withhis father and servant Ali and his son, Hassan. The two boys are separated from genuine brothers by their social level of friendship. Hassan admires and appreciates Amir is revered, and he even defends him from neighborhood bullies. Amir was twelve years old when he wins kite-flying competition, which, he hopes will bring him money and father's admiration.Throughout Amir's youth, he has had the impression that his father wishes for a manly son. Hassan assists Amir during the event by holding the spool while Amir works the strings and tries to cut the strings of his opponents' kites.

When Amir eventually cuts the remaining kite, Hassan, as promised, runs it down. Hassan does not return by dusk. Amir searches for him and discovers a new set of bullies harassing

Hassan. Assef, the group's leader, rapes Hassan while Amir watches from his hiding place, horrified. When he emerges from the alley with the kite, he runs part of the way home and pretends to meet Hassan for the first time.

Amir keeps the crime hidden and seeks to take advantage of Baba's attention. Guilt, on the other hand, has plagued him for years and has ruined his relationship with Hassan. Finally, he makes it appear that Hassan took his birthday money. Ali makes the decision. His son will also depart. As they drive away, Baba sobs. Amir and Baba are forced to flee Kabul because to political instability.

They ultimately arrive in America, where Baba, who was once wealthy, works as a gas station attendant. Amir completes high school and begins junior college. He falls in love with Soraya, an Afghan woman, and they marry barely a month before Baba passes away from lung cancer.

Rahim Khan, Baba's buddy and business partner in Kabul, calls with memories and a promise of forgiveness. Amir travels to Pakistan to see the man who is ill. He tells Amir about Hassan's arrival in Kabul, as well as Hassan's wife and kid. Hassan was slain in the streets by the Taliban months before Amir arrived in Pakistan. Rahim Khan also acknowledges that Baba is the father of Hassan, he is Amir's half-brother. Amir is startled by such information. Finally, he resolves to try to save Sohrab son of Hassan from an orphanage in Afghanistan.

The journey to Afghanistan turns out to be fateful. Amir hears that Assef now a strong Taliban figure, purchased Sohrab. Amir is challenged to a fight to the death. Assef nearly kills Amir before Sohrab, like his father always threatened, hits him with his slingshot. They make their way to Pakistan. They eventually arrive in Islamabad, where an American Embassy official informs Amir that Sohrab's adoption is hopeless. INS, Immigrations and Naturalization Services, relatives of Soraya control the strings.

However, before Amir can tell Sohrab, the boy becomes depressed and attempts suicide. He spends days in the ICU recovering. He eventually joins Amir on a flight to America. Soraya treats him as if he were the child they never had. Sohrab, on the other hand, remains silent. Finally, at an Afghan New Year's party, Amir floats a kite with his friends. Sohrab notices a glimmer of a smile. He chops down a competitor's kite and promises the same thing Hassan did twenty-six years ago.

A Thousand Splendid Suns, Hosseini's second novel, was published in May 2007. The novel is set in Afghanistan from the early 1960s to the early 2000s. Mariam is a little girl growing up in the 1960s outside of Herat, Afghanistan. Mariam's thoughts about her parents are complicated: Her mother, Nana, is cruel and stubborn, and her father, Jalil, a rich businessman, pays Mariam, his only illegitimate child on a weekly visit. Mariam resents her insignificant role in Jalil's life and wishes to live in Herat with him. For her sixteenth birthday, she expresses her hopes by requesting Jalil to take her to see Pinocchio. Jalil hesitantly agrees, but then fails to show up for the movie.

After her mother's death, Mariam is taken to Jalil's house. Jalil's wife doesn't want Mariam around, so they force her to marry Rasheed, a widowed shoemaker in Kabul. Rasheed first treats Mariam well, but after she has several miscarriages, he abuses her both physically and verbally. Rasheed's primary use for Mariam appears to be her potential to replace the son he lost years ago.

Laila, a young, intellectual girl from a loving family, grew up down the street from Rasheed and Mariam. However, Laila's youth is disrupted by the Afghani war against the Soviets, and both of her older brothers go to fight. Tariq, Laila's best friend and a boy offers her solace. Laila's parents learn that both of their sons have been slain just before she reaches adolescence. A few years later, the war has reached Kabul, and bombs are dropping on the city on a regular basis. Tariq and Laila are now adolescent lovers.Tariq informs Laila that he and his family are going to Pakistan, the couple makes their first passionate and rapid love. Laila's parents decide to leave Afghanistan a few days later, but while they pack, a rocket hits their house, killing Laila's parents and injuring her.

After Rasheed and Mariam have nursed Laila back to health, a stranger, Abdul Sharif, arrives to inform her that Tariq has died. Laila agrees to marry Rasheed after being devastated and learning she is pregnant with Tariq's child. Laila's presence initially hurts and threatens Mariam, and she refuses to interact with her.

After Laila gives birth to a baby, Aziza, the ladies begin to perceive themselves as allies in the face of Rasheed's harsh and manipulative behavior. Laila gives birth to a son, Zalmai, a few years later. After years of violence and despair, Laila is surprised to see a man standing at her front door one afternoon: Tariq.

While Rasheed is at work, Tariq and Laila spend the afternoon together. Rasheed recruited Abdul Sharif to tell Laila about Tariq's false death so she wouldn't flee. Rasheed savagely assaults Laila after he discovers Tariq has returned home. Mariam kills Rasheed with a shovel. The next day, Mariam surrenders to the Taliban in an attempt to clear the way for Laila and her children to seek refuge in Pakistan with Tariq.

Tariq and Laila marry in Pakistan, and finally start the life they've dreamed of for so long. Both of Laila's children eventually warmed up to Tariq and began to appreciate their new existence. However, their joy is overtaken by news that the United States had attacked Afghanistan in September 2001. Conditions in Kabul improve after the US invasion, and Laila insists that her family return home to help rebuild the city. On their way to Kabul, they stop at Herat, where Laila pays them a visit.Mariam's old home, where she is able to process her sadness over Mariam's death. Laila and Tariq start a new life in Kabul, where Laila teaches at the orphanage where Aziza used to live.And when Laila becomes pregnant, she decides that if she has a girl, she'll name her Mariam.

And the Mountains Echoed Hosseini's third novel, was published six years after his second novel. The form and narration of this work are both experimental. It includes a variety of unconnected stories that are only tangentially related to one another, forming the breadth of experiences of Afghan migrants around the world. Abdullah and Pari, brother and sister, are the key characters. Saboor, their father, is a senior citizen. He sells his small daughter to a couple in the city. Abdullah, who is saddened and never fully recovers from the blow of losing Pari. Mr. Wahdati and Nila, a Parisian couple, are given the name Pari. Nabi works for the couple and is smitten with Nila, but later discovers that Mr. Wahdati, who has suffered a stroke and is now paraplegic, was also smitten with Nabi. He was apparently a homosexual. He devotes the remainder of his life to Mr. Wahdati's care. Timur and Idris, Wahdati's relatives, live next door. After the conflict, they return to Afghanistan and interact with the locals. Idris encounters Roshi, a girl who was abused by terrorists and had her family murdered. She later migrates to the United States and writes a best-selling memoir on her ordeal in an Islamic country. Later Pari marries, and has three children. Nabi informs her that she was adopted from Saboor in a letter. She is ultimately reunited with her brother Abdullah, but he has Alzheimer's disease and does not know her. Pain, estrangement, suffering, death, and love are all themes explored in the novel.

The latest work of Hosseini Sea Prayer is composed in the form of a letter, from a father to his son on the eve of their journey. This powerful, illustrated book reflects current refugee crisis. Watching over his sleeping sun, the father reflects on the dangerous sea crossing that lies before them. Sea prayer is also a vivid portrait of their life in Homs, Syria, before the war, and of that city's swift transformation from a home into a horrific and bloody war zone.

Social conflict theory is a Marxist-based social theory which argues that individuals and groups (social classes) within society interact on the basis of conflict rather than consensus. Through various forms of conflict, groups will tend to attain differing amounts of material and non-material resources (the wealthy vs. the poor, etc). More powerful groups will tend to use their power in order to retain power and exploit groups with less power. Conflict theory has sought to explain a wide range of social phenomena, including wars, revolutions, poverty, discrimination, and domestic violence. It ascribes most of the fundamental developments in human history, such as democracy and civil rights, to capitalistic attempts to control the masses (as opposed to a desire for social order). Central tenets of conflict theory are the concepts of social inequality, the division of resources, and the conflicts that exist among different socioeconomic classes.

The chapters following focuses on the social structure of Afghanistan and how it affects the life of marginalized people.

# CHAPTER TWO

# SOCIAL STRUCTURE OF AFGHANISTAN

Literature is an output of writer's interaction with society and social environment shape his creativity. Contemporary political, social, cultural and religious tendencies are always articulated in the literary creations. Literary creativity being a product of its age, always needs a comprehensive understanding of its background. Age-old religious fanaticism, cruel social practices and contemporary political chaos play a significant role in influencing the contemporary literary output. Survival becomes especially unique in a country like Afghanistan where threats to life and violence are in profusion. The country has been used as a battlefield for a long time by external powers. Its geographic position is the main cause for this; Afghanistan is an entirely landlocked country situated in the southern part of Asia and is located in the east of Iran and north and west of Pakistan, sharing boarder with Turkmenistan, Uzbekistan, Tajikistan and China. Afghanistan has abundant natural resources, but the country is known only as a source of opium. From the economic viewpoint, Afghanistan is considered among the poorest and the least developed countries in the world and is categorized as a 'Third World Country'.

Afghanistan is a landlocked country with different ethnic groups ruling different regions. Ethnic conflicts are prevalent in regional politics and are frequently related with violence, discrimination, and other forms of discrimination. As well as a variety of significant human rights violations since over three decades, Afghanistan has been devastated, driving millions of people to flee their homes. Armed ethnic groups allowed governmental control to rest in their hands that have grown accustomed to acting with near-total impunity as a result of constant exposure conflicts. As a result, women in Afghanistan are the most disadvantaged and destitute group, with gender equality and women's independence still a long way of domestic abuse, rape, sex trafficking, domestic slavery, the sale of an infant girl, and unequal opportunity and remuneration in the workplace are all frequent. Local leaders continue to impose Taliban-style restrictions on women in various parts of the country.

The relentless conflicts of the late 20th and 21st century have produced generations of Afghans who have rarely experienced peace. They have resisted invasions from Great Britain and the Soviet Union, and continue to persevere despite the ongoing insurgency by the Taliban and others. Consequently, many Afghans think of themselves as survivors. Further, people are often strongly opposed to outside interference in internal politics. This has translated into a prevailing national attitude that strongly favors independence from controlling bodies. However, the assertion of the country's independence has not necessarily resulted in national cohesiveness. Afghans tend to hold a stronger sense of loyalty for their kin, tribe or ethnicity than their national identity.

In Afghan society, men's supreme power over their families (or women) is seen as important for maintaining social order. When women deviate from established methods of behaving, carrying themselves, and living, it is seen as a sign of social breakdown. It is thought that in order to maintain male pride and honor, the man must have influence over feminine behavior decisions. Even among modern families, this type of idea is still prevalent.

One's ethnicity is an instant cultural identifier in Afghanistan and usually defines people's social organisation. The most common ethnic groups are the Pashtuns, Tajiks and Hazaras. However, there are also significant populations of Uzbeks, Nuristani, Aimak,

Turkmen and Baloch.

The Pashtun are the largest ethnic group in Afghanistan. Most speak Pashto and are Sunni Muslims. Pashtun culture and social organisation have been traditionally influenced by tribal codes of honour and interpretations of Islamic law. This is recognised as 'Pashtunwali' – a moral and legal code that determines the social expectations one should follow to honour Islamic and cultural values. Pashtunwali, in its strictest form, is mostly only followed in rural tribes. However, its influence can still be seen in much of Pashtun behaviour. For example, values such as honour, loyalty, hospitality and protection of female relatives remain important principles of social responsibility throughout Afghanistan.

The Pashtun are widely regarded as the most politically influential and dominant group in Afghanistan. Successive governments have formed via the political expansion of Pashtun tribes with international assistance. Members of minority ethnicities have argued that the national identity of the country is exclusionary of non-Pashtun ethnicities. Afghanistan actually means Land of the Pashtun in Dari. Indeed, Afghan exclusively referred to Pashtuns before it came to refer to the citizens of the state.

Nevertheless, while Pashtuns have continuously held advantage in the political domain, many do not see or receive the privileges that come from being a member of the most dominant ethnic group. Political power and economic wealth definitively lies in the hands of the few. Many Pashtuns earn subsistence-level or very modest incomes as traders, farmers, livestock breeders and merchants.

The Tajiks have Persian heritage and are Afghanistan's second largest ethnicity. Unlike most other ethnicities, they are not tribal and do not organise themselves by tribal association. Instead, their loyalty revolves around their family and village (or local community for those living in urban areas). This is evident in the way many Tajik last names tend to reflect their place of origin, rather than their tribe or ethnicity.

Tajiks are majority Sunni Muslim and generally speak a dialect of Persian found in Eastern Iran. The Tajiks tend to be more urbanised than many other ethnicities and are relatively less rigid in their adherence to provincial attitudes. Some reside in Kabul or the north-eastern part of the country. Many also live in the west, close to the Iranian border. Those who live in the cities are usually traders or skilled artisans. However, the majority are farmers and herders.

Tajiks commonly have a high level of education and wealth (in comparison to some of Afghanistan's more impoverished ethnicities), which has seen them be widely considered to be among Afghanistan's elite. According to Minority Rights Group International, this accumulated privilege gives them quite a high social status as an ethnic group. However, the Tajik political influence is not very dominant. Many Tajiks have been persecuted amidst the unrest of the past 35 years and discussions over their political representation in government continue.

The Hazara people are widely understood to be one of the most socially and politically marginalised ethnic groups in Afghanistan. They speak a dialect of Dari known as Hazaragiand make up the largest Shi'a Muslim population in the country. Most Hazaras live in the central mountain region and in certain districts of Kabul.

The Hazaras have been persecuted by Pashtun leaders, civil warlords, the Taliban, ISIS and others due to their Shi'a Muslim beliefs. For example, government policies have excluded them from public service and capped their ranks in the military. This has resulted in their systemic lack of political power and influence in a Sunni Muslim majority country. The persecution of Hazaras has been particularly fierce as they have hereditary features (from distant Mongol ancestry) that physically distinguish their ethnicity from other Afghans.

Many Hazaras have lived through raids and massacres of their people, both in past and recent years. Some have escaped this danger in neighbouring Pakistan where other Sunni extremists have also sought to target and kill them. Consequently, many have been left with no choice but to flee to more distant countries. As a result, a large portion of the Afghans in Western countries are Hazara refugees who have sought asylum from this situation.

The Hazarajat region remains very poor, meaning many Hazaras are economically supported by a male family member who has journeyed to a city or neighbouring country to find work. Being at the bottom of the economic and social hierarchy has also stigmatised Hazaras in the minds of most other ethnic groups. This is acutely reflected in the lack of inter-ethnic marriages with Hazaras. Nevertheless, more recently, Hazaras have been pursuing higher education and political positions to represent their people and become leaders in the newly emerging democracy.

The Taliban not only used terror to acquire political power, but they were also known for their treatment of women and children, as well as their draconian rules. The Taliban imposed the hejab as a basic requirement for women, based on their interpretation of Muslim law. Women must be fully clothed from head to toe whenever they go outside. Islamic law considers the hejab to be more dignified than the chador, which exposes the facial arc. The Taliban's interpretation of the shariyat requires women to wear Afghan burqas: a head to toe garment that must cover almost every inch of a woman's body and is quite different from the Pakistani or Iranian type of burqa, in which the face and eyes are exposed.

Women were forbidden from working, and their primary responsibility was to bear and rear Afghanistan's future generations. Because women were to be confined to their homes and the majority of elementary teachers in Afghan schools were women, many schools were burned or closed. Women were subjected to physical and mental torture for minor reasons. Women who were assaulted were frequently unable to seek medical help since male doctors were not permitted to treat women unless they were accompanied by a male family member. The Taliban eventually allowed some female doctors to work, but only on the condition that they wear the burqa.

Men were not exempt from such barbarisms and horrors just because women had to endure a long period of brutality and humiliation. Men were compelled to grow beards and told to dress appropriately in public. They made it mandatory to wear salwar, or baggy, ankle-length trousers. As a result, the dress code also represents the restriction of men's freedoms. The announcement for men:

While the Taliban may have begun calling shots with good intentions, Osama Bin Laden's entry in Afghanistan in 1996 changed the Taliban's future dramatically. Taliban has been designated as a terrorist organization. The organization was suspected of routinely assisting Bin Laden and his Al-Qaeda network. Following the attacks on the World Trade Center in New York and the Pentagon in Washington, D.C. on September 11, 2001, the United States acted quickly and ruthlessly against terrorist groups led by the Taliban.The Taliban had been deposed from power in Afghanistan before the end of 2001. Plans were developed in the following months to form a new democratic administration in Afghanistan. US military forces start to control Afghanistan. Karzai was also chosen interim president in Loya Jigra in 2002, and elections were held in 2004. Literature reflected every facet of Afghan life in the midst of such chaos and violence. It continued to scream forth the silent cries of those who were suffering.

By the end of 2018, the US was determined to completing the withdrawal, placing President Ashraf Ghani's Afghan government under pressure from a resurgent Taliban.

The Afghan government made a big admission in January 2019. It claimed to have lost around 45,000 security personnel in the previous five years, under Ashraf Ghani's presidency and the Taliban's comeback. The Trump administration, on the other hand, was adamant on returning US troops from Afghanistan. Following numerous rounds of negotiations in Qatar, the US and the Taliban reached an agreement in February 2020. The US and NATO were supposed to pull out of Afghanistan in a certain amount of time. Afghanistan has been devastated by the US-Taliban conflict. In this war-torn country, the Taliban had no trouble finding recruits or funds for their operations. In Afghanistan, Pakistani madrasas and Islamic seminaries continued to supply jihadi fighters. The Taliban benefited from the opposition to American occupation in Afghanistan.

# CHAPTER THREE

# SOCIAL ISSUES IN THE NOVEL KITE RUNNER

The Kite Runner was published in 2003 and became a best seller as early as 2005. The novel made readers aware of the sufferings faced by people in Afghanistan, which had been unreachable to outsiders for a long time. Through this novel, Hosseini seeks to show that Afghanistan is more than simply the Soviet invasion, the Taliban, and American intervention; it also represents various forms of life in the midst of multi-layered harsh situations. From the darkness of anonymity, he succeeds in showcasing the ordinary Afghan people in all aspects of their lives. Via comprehensive human narrative, the novel refocuses the attention of Afghanistan through a different lens, rectifying the restricted image of Afghanistan that has a fascinating past. Through this novel, Hosseini reveals the actual colors of Afghan culture, customs, traditions, taboos, social structure, political, and religious beliefs. The faulty and inaccurate picture of Afghan people as simple "bearded gunmen" is shattered in Hosseini's work.

The Kite Runner depicts Afghanistan in the 1970s at one of its most calm periods in its history. Amir, the son of a wealthy businessman in Kabul, and Hassan, the son of Amir's household worker Ali, who lives in a mud-sac hut in the corner of Amir's villa, are good friends.Hassan is a Shia Muslim who belongs to the Hazara community, which is viewed as an 'ethnically inferior' group in the Afghan socio-cultural environment. Amir is a Sunni Muslim who belongs to the Pasthuns, an 'ethnically superior' sect of Afghanistan. Amir and Hassan grew up together on the tranquil streets of Kabul, playing, laughing, and flying kites. A single day changes the course of all the characters' lives, forcing them to fight for survival in their own unique ways. Hassan goes to deliver the kite after Amir wins a kite-flying competition, but a local bully named Assef viciously beats him in an empty street. Amir is seeing everything through a small hole, but he is too weak to help his faithful friend. Amir and Hassan become strangers as a result of this incident. Amir grows tired of Hassan, imposes his own weakness on him, and fails to confront him. Amir covertly puts his watch and some cash in Hassan's bed one day.Later on, he accuses Hassan of theft and pushes his father and Ali to split up.

In The Kite Runner, Amir is the main character who represents an ideal survival in real-life situations. He possesses a wide range of characteristics, both good and negative, and uses them all effectively for his survival as and when required. His character is complex that defies easy analysis because he is a mix of several characteristics. His early attributes can be listed as liar, envious, submissive, betrayer, and coward, but he eventually transforms into a bold, confident, sincere, honest, and loyal person. In this way, The Kite Runner depicts the protagonist's personal growth. In some ways, this voyage mimics Hosseini's autobiography. Amir does not exhibit heroic qualities early in the story, but he eventually develops them. On both an emotional and exterior level, he fights his circumstances. Amir is still beset by various disputes and fears. He's having trouble connecting with his father and is dealing with recollections of a traumatic childhood event. In his early years, he faces rejection from his father and observes several violent episodes. His father despises him because his mother died shortly after he was born. He accuses him for not being a rough, sturdy, and pugnacious Pashtun lad because he does not provide him enough love and care. Always Baba compares him withHassan, his illegitimate brother. Amir overhears Baba's words to Rahim.

"Sometimes I look out this window and see him playing with the kids on the street," Khan says. Boys from the surrounding I observe how they push him around, take his toys away from him, and make fun of him. A whack here and there he never fights back, you know never. He simply drops his head" (Hosseini 19).

Amir gets deeply hurt when Baba rejects him saying that "there is something missingin that boy" (20). Amir's ambiguous and obscure nature is a characteristic which has been abnormally instilled in him by Baba's rejection of him due to some irrational reasons. Amir is perplexed and disturbed as a result of his father's disappointing and critical statements. Amir believes that such remarks make him feel insecure in his own home. He is unable to reason with his father, and his mental turmoil causes him to fantasize about his own universe. He imagines himself undertaking adventurous acts that persuade his father to reward him with love and care while daydreaming. Even in his fantasies, recognition from his father becomes a desire and a 'goal' for him to achieve.In real life, though, he is too afraid to undertake such heroic acts. He devises several defence mechanisms to avoid psychological stress and strain in such tense situations. He ignores reality and withdraws from real-life situations in his fantasies. These defence mechanisms provide him with ample time and space to mentally prepared to deal with the assaults and barriers. He mentally prepares himself to overcome the obstacles, but in such a complex setting, he crosses the line of reason. Gradually, he loses his defences and learns to deal with events rationally and tactfully. As a form of self-defense, he deploys the projection mechanism. Hassan is the target of Baba's rejection and emotional aggression.He plots violence against Hassan since he considers him subservient and harmless. He sees Hassan as a roadblock to receiving respect, affection, and care from Baba, so he chooses to kick him out of his house and life. Amir becomes a criminal and devious guy as a result of Baba's disapproval. He successfully identifies Hassan a thief and eliminates him for good.

"Then I took a few of envelops of cash from the pile of gifts and my watch," Amir informs Soraya. I entered Ali and Hassan's living quarters by going downstairs and crossing the yard. "I lifted Hassan's mattress and placed my new watch and a few Afghani bills beneath it" (90).

Because of Amir's betrayal of Hassan, he feels ashamed and terrible, and he finds himself in even more pitiful circumstances. His mental issues suffocate him, and he longs for a tranquil existence. He laments not being able to stop Hassan from being sodomized and condemns himself for kicking him out. Amir is encumbered with his own knowledge that in the past he didn't help his friend because he is jealous of him as well as being cowardly. This sense of guilt develops into a long-term source of psychological distress in his life.

Amir's embrace of truth forces him to reflect on his previous transgressions. He feels guilty and repents whenever he recalls Hassan's rape and elimination:

"I looked at the round face in the Polaroid again, the way the sun fell on it.Face of my brother. Hassan had once loved me in a manner that no one else had or would ever love me again. He was no longer with us, but a small part of him remained. It happened in Kabul" (199).

When Amir is exposed to his deeply internalized memories, his unhealed mind bleeds. Amir is haunted by the painful recollections even on his happiest days in America. He has an internal conflict that drives him to atone for his wrongdoings and redeem his past. It always irritates him that his convenience comes at the expense of Hassan's dignity. He does not consider this existence to be genuine; he repeatedly recalls his inability to save Hassan and adds,

"I had one last chance to make a decision." I had one more chance to select who I wanted to be... I could walk into that alley stand up for Hassan the way he'd always stood up for me" (69).

In the latter portion of his life, Amir's surrender and acceptance of his own previous sins transforms him. Rather than succumbing to bullying or awful behaviour, he resolves to fight back. He resolves to engage in more aggressive confrontation with reality right away. He learns to be loyal to himself and others. He is confident and trustworthy since he accepts and submits his own wrongdoings. He now quickly resolves his internal conflicts. In truth, his self-assurance stems from his departure from Afghanistan, a hotbed of violence, to America and the difficulties he encountered during his exile. The arrival of Soviet and his subsequent flight educate him to bear the anguish of losses. He is now experiencing the pain of having to leave his house. He also realizes that his past self-defense techniques of repression, regression, suppression, rejection, and projection are only a temporary escape from reality that, in the long run, renders him incapable of acting. He admits that a person must be able to deal with both internal and external threats. He admits that in a situation like to Afghanistan, bloodshed is unavoidable. He imagines that in order to withstand extreme violence, one must suffer it and, if necessary, retaliate in self-defense. Excessive flight, suppression, or rejection over an extended period of time just adds to the size of fear and anxiety.

Through Hassan, Hosseini depicts various sorts of violence endured by Afghan youngsters, particularly ethnic minorities. Hassan has been the victim of both self-directed interpersonal and collective violence. In the narrative, he is subjected to all kind of heinous violence, including physical, sexual, emotional, and psychic. Hassanemphasizes the concept of sacrifice, obedience, and subjugation, which is portrayed through the image of a lamb. A thorough investigation reveals that ethnic discrimination, which has long existed in Afghan society, is the primary cause of his persecution. It escalates and accentuates, deeply multilayered and highly multifaceted, in the harsh conditions of unending wars, terrorism, and fundamentalism. Hassan's victimization is so complicated and intertwined that it's practically difficult for him to survive. Hassan, on the other hand, possesses some distinct characteristics and demonstrates remarkable courage in the face of adversity. It is due to his tenacious determination that he maintains his life even in the face of life-threatening circumstances. In his fictitious story, Hosseini depicts many forms of prejudice and various survival methods used by the victims, depending on the circumstances in Afghanistan. Despite the fact that the story is told by Amir, a Pashtun by ethnicity, it deals with a variety of extraordinary trials and tribulations endured by three generations of the same family, symbolic of the trials and tribulations endured by thousands of Hazara people over the years in their struggle to survive.

According to Hosseini, the struggle for existence in Afghanistan is not a uniform phenomenon. It varies depending on the sect and gender. The situation of ethnic minorities who arc openly discriminated against is appalling and depressing. The downtrodden bear the brunt of the burden of maintaining social bonds, which makes life even more difficult for them. Amir breaks the link of friendship, which is at the heart of the story; he appears to have no regard for social institutions such as friendship, whereas Hassan is forced to go through hardships in order to keep his friendship. In social interactions and history, hierarchies have a vital role in intensifying discrimination. To the oppressed, hierarchy appears natural; following it is simpler than rebelling against it. Any oppressive system strives to identify its origins in history for justification and reinforcement. Once introduced, it is passed along from generation to generation, making its elimination nearly impossible. As a result, the fight against discrimination is a long and exhausting one.

Hassan's struggle and Amir's struggle are clearly separated by Hosseini. He claims that for people like Hassan, survival is a long-term process because whereas ethnically superior people must resist foreign invasions, the destitute and oppressed must always face sufferings caused by their own countrymen. Hassan assists his father with household chores while Amir attends a reputable school in Kabul. Baba and Ali never discuss Hassan's educational prospects. It implies that Hazaras are illiterate and are solely expected to work as servants. Hassan is denied his fundamental right to education, a form of abuse used to force him to live the life of a servant. Hassan, on the other hand, is a natural genius who possesses innate abilities and excels at poetry and riddles. Amir despises his intelligence. He frequently makes ethnic remarks about Hassan, such as, "What does that ignorant Hazara know? He'll never be more than a cook. He doesn't have any right to criticize me" (30). In Amir's life, Hassan is like a toy. When others (Pashtun) are present, Amir does not include Hassan in games. In actuality, Hassan is not his friend, but rather a servant who, as Amir says, "play the part of a friend as commanded for a while" (36). As a result, Hassan is constantly subjected to interpersonal aggression by his master's son.

In the novel, Assef, a sociopath, is the embodiment of evil. He was born in Germany to a Pashtun father and a German mother. He is more extremist and obsessive on ethnic issues than any of the 'pure' Pashtuns. He appears to admire Hitler and compares Hitler's hatred for Jews to his own animosity for Hazaras. Amir's prejudice against Hassan is limited to his thoughts and words, as he likes him to some extent, whereas Assef reacts terribly to Hazaras. He has a visceral hatred for Hazaras, which he expresses in his words,

"Afghanistan is the land of Pashtuns..., We are true Afghans, pure Afghans, not this snobbish bunch here; his people poison our homelands, our watan.I say Afghanistan for Pashtuns because they taint our blood. That's how I see things... Hitler was too late... However, not for us... I'll ask the President to get rid of all the filthy Kasseef Hazaras in Afghanistan" (35).

It's worth noting that Hassan is just as Pashtun as Assef and is more Afghan. Hassan is the son of a Pashtun father (Baba) and an Afghan mother, but Assef's mother is German; the only difference is that Assef is acknowledged as Pashtun, however Hassan is not because he is an illegitimate child. As a result of his illegitimacy, he is denied the right to be a Pashtun, and as a Hazara, he faces violent persecution. It implies that force is always right. Power concentration makes life difficult for those on the margins. Power incites aggression against the weak and their lives become a never-ending battle against the brutality and oppression imposed on them without thought.

Assef rapes Hassan because he is a Hazara and justifies himself saying: "And there is nothing sinful about teaching a lesson to a disrespectful donkey . . . It's just a Hazara" (66). Assef's visceral hostility shows that the ideas instilled in childhood grow stronger with time. Prejudices turn into beliefs. These ingrained prejudices embitter the mind so much that social fabric is torn asunder and disastrous consequences follow. In Afghanistan, oppression and prejudice are unavoidably practiced on a daily basis. Both the suppressor and the suppressed regard it as natural. The suppressor enjoys it, while the suppressed must endure it in order to survive. They must succumb to oppression and prejudice because the situation is too severe for them to opposehaphazardly in order to exist and survive. In Afghanistan, there is widespread socio-ethnic discrimination.

Afghan children face a slew of challenges, including high infant mortality rates, child labors, child marriage, malnutrition, and the loss of parents, a pitiful existence in orphanages, begging, and being victims of extremist ideology pursued by terrorists and jihadis, and, above all, child sexual assault. Pedophilia, a persistent and exclusive sexual attraction toward young and innocent children, is one of the most well-known types of child sexual abuse. In Afghanistan, pedophilia is mostly expressed through bachabazi, a disparaging phrase that means playing with a boy. Playing represents a male child's multiple victimizations. It is possible to define it as an interaction between an innocent youngster and a bachabazi or pedophile that results in horrific bodily and psychological consequences. It's a form of male child prostitution and sexual enslavement perpetrated by wealthy or powerful males for their own entertainment and to satisfy their warped sexual desires.

Hosseini brilliantly conveys the bachabazi dilemma through Sohrab. Sohrab is Hassan and Farzana's kid, and he looks and acts remarkably identically like Hassan. He represents third-generation persecution. Even after death, he appears to be the embodiment of Hassan's plight. After the Taliban brutally murder Hassan and Farzana, innocent Sohrab is sent to an orphanage. However, life in the orphanage turns out to be a nightmare for him. The orphanage's director, Zaman, is a kind and gentle guy, yet he is powerless to save Sohrab from his fate. Through the interaction of Sohrab and pedophilic Assef, Hosseini reveals vulgar, and obnoxious form of bachabazi. Sohrab is introduced as,

"Aboydressed in a loose sapphire blue pirhan-tumban. His eyes darkened with mascara,and his cheeks glowed with an unnatural red . . . The bells strapped around his ankletsstopped" (244).

Bachabazihas been a tradition in Afghanistan, and in keeping with the custom, Sohrab is made to dance like a woman,

"He stood on tiptoes, spun gracefully,dipped at his knees, straightened, and spun again. His little hands swiveled at his wrists,his fingers snapped, and his head swung side to side like a pendulum. His feet poundedthe floor" (245).

Sohrab's activities suggest that he has grown trained and accustomed to dancing, as well as that the bachabazi problem is not a new one, as it is intergenerational and conventional. Poor children have always been sex toys, only to be humiliated, as each generation abuses the next in a spontaneous and cyclic manner. Because a man of great rank is rarely hampered or prevented by societal or legal pressures or limits, power plays a crucial part in the victimization of children. The impoverished and innocent are always considered as property or as a source of pleasure. Powerful men do not require stealth; they openly flaunt their privileges and disregard society's conventions and guiding principles. Assef, a high-ranking Taliban official, freely and brazenly expresses his pedophilic tendencies. In Amir's presence, his behavior becomes even more perverted as he overreacts:

"'Bia, bia, my boy...'encircled the youngster with his arms. He exclaimed, 'How talented he is, nay, my Hazara boy!' he ran his hands down the child's back, then up, feeling beneath his armpits"

(245).

Khaled Hosseini portrays the bachabazi dilemma honestly and sympathetically, showing it as a part of the several layers of survival struggle. Any media coverage, case study or history book cannot compare to the treatment of the problem. He also mentions child labor, begging, poverty, malnutrition, illiteracy, fundamentalism, and even the practice of circumcision as issues facing Afghan children. All of these issues are linked and may be traced back to fanaticism, terrorism, and conflict. A slew of issues make children's lives sad beyond belief, and their struggle to stay alive is particularly difficult.

Hosseini does not gloss over any aspect of Afghanistan's children's lives. A child's survival in Afghanistan is riddled with difficulties. Sohrab's death represents the deaths of thousands of Afghan children. Sohrab is capable of not only overcoming obstacles, but also of making sacrifices and adapting to terrifying and difficult conditions. When Assef treats him badly, he adjusts, but when he has a chance, he retaliates for his survival. This demonstrates that Sohrab is a tough guy on the inside, and he has not succumbed to the sexual assault for good; rather, he was patiently waiting to strike back and escape humiliation and indignity.

Baba is a typical Afghan figure who takes pride in their culture, ancestry, religion, and, most importantly, their independence. He is also an example of a struggle for survival. He is not exposed to many forms of violence, but he is constantly preoccupied with anxiety as a result of his internal problems. Baba is a sufferer of self-inflicted violence, which he projects onto his son Amir at times and tries to alleviate his tension by giving money to beggars at other times. He is always plagued by moral uneasiness and overtaken by his own sense of shame as a result of his past sins. His life is plagued by guilt and moral worry, and he appears to be fighting these issues throughout the novel in order to find authenticity and significance. He has become neurotic on a psychological level as a result of burying his secrets and guilt feelings for so long. He is tired of hiding his secrets due to social pressure and tries to reduce the severity of his past wrongdoings by performing selfless acts for the disadvantaged and disenfranchised, as well as releasing his rage on his son. Baba feels very sorry for cheating on his wife and having an illegitimate son with his servant's wife, Hassan. He believes himself responsible for his wife's premature death. He blames his wife's suffering on his own sins, although he doesn't say so but freely express it Baba wants to demonstrate his love for Hassan, his illegitimate son, but the Afghan social structure and his personal reputation prevent him from doing so. Hassan is now regarded as a Hazara lad, a member of a lower race, which grieves Baba much. Baba feels suffocated from the inside out, and his life has become a living hell. He attempts in vain to find a resolution to his inner issues in order to breathe in peace.

He is often so disturbed and overwhelmed by the problem that he loses his mind, but he quickly recovers by burying his secrets and problems. He attempts to treat Hassan like a son by treating him the same as Amir. He buys Hassan the same gifts he gives Amir, and he takes the children to the market and on a picnic. From the window, he keeps an eye on Hassan and notices that Hassan has inherited more of his characteristics than Amir. Due to his moral inadequacy, Baba faces internal struggles. Baba has clearly spent only half of his life with Amir, while the other half of his life has been buried in Hassan.

Due to Russian invasion, Baba flees to America with Amir, leaving behind all of his land and the royal life he had led. However, he expends a lot of work settling here and adapting to the American way of life. He makes an admirable effort to live a better expatriate life with good pay. In the presence of Amir, his demeanour changes to charming and cautious, as the two of them had shared horrific life experiences. He provides Amir complete autonomy and cooperation in choosing his partner and job. He believes that granting freedom is a gift. Baba is a dedicated worker who takes on strange jobs that do not suit his nature. He misses Hassan and Ali throughout his existence in America and imagines their presence all around him. He manages not only his own life in exile, but also all of his responsibilities to Amir and his wife.

He is not afraid during his illness; rather, he shows courage in facing the final trials of his life, and he struggles inside until his death to reach his 'half'. In a word, Baba embodies the attributes of a survivor: he maintains his dignity while maintaining an aristocratic life, but he is forced to move to America due to his and Amir's lives being threatened, and he lives a respectable life there as well.

Other minor characters in the narrative also go through enormous trials and tribulations in life. Amir and Hassan have a family buddy named Rahim Khan. In the story, he appears to personify 'goodness.' He assists all of the characters in the narrative in leading calm lives. He is equally a companion to Baba and Amir. However, the novelist does not go into great detail about Rahim Khan's character, but there are a few details that demonstrate how he patiently controls his life. He is a strong man who refuses to leave Afghanistan, even after the Soviet invasion and the arrival of the Taliban, preferring instead to live in solitary. Hosseini is brutal in his portrayal of Ali. He has been stripped of all of his rights. Hazara is his birth name. He is physically and sexually impaired. His wife and brother-like master betrayed him, and the rest of the neighborhood mocks him. But he is determined and has a good outlook on life. Love, goodness, and loyalty are values he holds dear. He accepts problems with grace and spends his life with patience and fortitude, never complaining. As a Hazara and a servant, he understands his limitations. As a result, his boss treats him as a brother. His fight for survival serves as an example to Afghanistan's poor and minority populations. Hassan's love provides him with a source of energy. He is willing to put up with everything for the sake of Hassan's betterment. That is why, in order to protect Hassan, he decides to abandon Baba's house and career and live a life of poverty and hunger in his paternal village.Throughout his quest for survival, Ali demonstrates exceptional tolerance, patience, and compromise.

Throughout the story, there are several scenes that depict various acts of violence and survivor stories. Life in Afghanistan was peaceful prior to the Soviet invasion, although interpersonal violence, ethnic prejudice, and violence against women and children have always existed. In terms of women's roles in society, the Afghan social structure is exceedingly conservative and narrow-minded, and any attempt by women to assert themselves and break free from the limits of family life has always been met with harsh resistance and violence. However, after the Soviet invasion, violence erupted in Afghanistan, and The Kite Runner vividly depicts the various forms of heinous brutality and various survival techniques used by Afghans. The entire scenario depicted by Hosseini in the novel gives the impression that not only a few groups but also ordinary people are fighting to survive in the highly volatile conditions; rather, Afghanistan as a whole has been fighting to maintain its unity against the onslaught of divisive forces from within and without.

# CHAPTER FOUR

# OPPRESSION AGAINST WOMEN IN A THOUSAND SPLENDID SUNS

A Thousand Splendid Suns is a novel of women's oppression and howdespite the odds, there is still hope for them; that there is still humanity left in the world's darkest corners. In a religious theocracy like Afghanistan, there is little hope for women, but the optimism that exists should be picked up and worked on, at least that is Khaled Hosseini's message in A Thousand Splendid Suns. Even in the face of adversity, the novel's protagonists, notably the ladies, maintain hope. They bear the persecution of men, society, religion and continue to hope that their situation may be improved one day. Though their circumstances are oppressive, the protagonists exhibit hope at several key points in the works.

A Thousand Splendid Suns is set in Afghanistan between 1960 and 2000 and spans four decades. It begins with the description of a middle-aged woman who works as a poor maid at Jalil's house and is sexually exploited by Jalil, a wealthy man of Heart. She suffers in silence because society is unkind to her. She is given no identity and is left alone in a little cottage to suffer. She isfinancially weak and is reliant on Jalil's weekly assistance. She is subjected to humiliations.Jalil's family and society do not accept her. She is so miserable that she takes her own life. Emotional collapse and seclusion her death reveals patriarchal society's oppression and deception. Morality and Afghan culture prevent abandoned women from exercising their right to life. Mariam recalls the situation: "there is only one skill a woman. She must have tahamul endure" (17).

In all of his writings, Hosseini has addressed the struggle of women. Women are compelled to obey and tolerate their husbands' persecution. They were transformed to child-bearing robots under Taliban regulations. The prominent character of the work Mariam who married to Rasheed don't have a happy life. When Mariam has multiple miscarriages, Rasheed transforms into a terrible monster who torments and tortures the helpless Mariam.Rasheed believes in patriarchal tyranny and tells Mariam that she is naturally docile and subservient. To please her husband, she obeys him and agrees to wear a burqa. Her slave existence and loss of vision are symbolized by her burqa. Rasheed is an orthodox Muslim who is illiterate and from the working class. His worldview is restricted, he tortures Mariam physical and verbally. Rasheed has no feelings for Mariam; all he wants is for her to have a son.

Mariam is oppressed; she is confined to a dark chamber where she must endure agony and suffering. Mariam has been beaten cruelly; her hair has been torn and she has been thrashed mercilessly. All female characters in this work Nana, Mariam, and Laila have all been beaten, raped, and sexually assaulted. They are tortured physically and psychologically. They are subjugated by sexism, terrorism, and the Taliban's religious extremism. Because of Taliban terrorism and Afghanistan's political instability, Laila loses Tariq and her parents. For the first time, the Taliban introduced gun culture to Afghanistan. They enacted stringent legislation prohibiting all forms of entertainment. Nobody was allowed to perform music, and publishing books and watching movies were prohibited.

As the Taliban degraded everyone, the biggest peril was to young girls as well as adults. Life of Mariam also pathetic. Rasheedignores Mariam, who lives the life of a married widow. She is a very unfortunate young lady, as her wealthy father ignores her and her husband abuses her. Her miscarriages become the true source of her suffering. Laila is a well-educated young woman, but the war wrecked her family and her life. Rasheed is a selfish and greedy individualdesiresLaila. Because Mariam turns out to be a barren woman, Rasheed marries Laila. Laila was forced to marry Rasheed after her parents were slain in the battle. Her fate is intertwined with Mariam's. Both are victims of Taliban atrocities. Laila is expecting her first child with Tariq, who relocated to Pakistan to escape Taliban terror. Mariam's troubles began with the arrival of Laila. Rasheed loses interest in Mariam and refuses to sleep with her, causing Mariam to feel alienated. Laila has a child and is surrounded by Rasheed's love and trust. But this devotion is self-centered, as he soon begins abusing her.

Mariam builds a positive relationship with Laila as she searches for a purpose in life. Her major goal is to watch after Laila's children and save her from Rasheed's cruelty.Rasheed feels envious of Laila, who is deeply in love with Tariq. Rasheed is guilty because he told Laila a series of lies concerning Tariq's death. Rasheed intends to murder Laila since she is in love with Tariq. The Taliban imposed stringent laws that granted Rasheed unlimited power. All women's rights were taken away. The Taliban's severe policies have forced Mariam and Laila to endure. When the Taliban forbade women from leaving their houses, a cultural clash arose. They were not permitted to leave the building. Because they are not allowed to work, Mariam and Laila are forced to live in Rasheed's cage. Laila was raised in a liberal environment, but in Rasheed's house, she is trapped in a cage to suffer indefinitely. Rasheed is a ruthless husband who believes in authoritarian patriarchy.Rashid intimidates Mariam by saying, "I know you're shaking!" Have I scared you? 'Do I terrify you? 'Do you have any fear of me?' (60). Mariam's life is a living misery, as she is constantly harassed by

Rasheed. It was difficult to spend time with Rasheed because of his volatile disposition. Rashid would get sadistic satisfaction from humiliating and beating Mariam. Wounds on her delicate body were nothing new to her, but she had hardened and toughened with time. Rasheed used to beat his women severely and was a horror in the house.

After the death of Nana Mariam is left alone to confront the brutal world. She discovers the realities of life and human interactions for the first time when she discovers her father to be a giant hypocrite since she is forced to sleep outside her father's large mansion. She remembers her mother's comments and curses her for disobeying her. According to the Bible, disobedience is the root of all human misery. Mariam feels guilty and is constantly bothered by it. She believes she is to blame for her mother's death via suicide. She has no choice but to accept her nasty father's marriage proposal because she has nowhere else to go. Jalil had treated her inhumanely. He had numerous contacts in the family and might have married her in a good family. Laila, on the other hand, is hastily married to a much older cobbler. The novel's plot is set against the backdrop of political turmoil and Taliban authority. Afghanistan was decimated by the Taliban, and people continued to suffer. The cultural changes in society have a negative impact on Laila, Tariq, and Mariam. Laila believes in the rebirth of her country, but she is enraged by the sight of the warlords going away with their heads held high.

Mariam was caught in a cultural maelstrom when she had to confront Rasheed, who represented traditional Muslim culture. She fought to survive in Kabul's war-torn society. Mariam is always plagued by feelings of guilt. She believes she is to blame for her mother's death. Nana's death was no ordinary occurrence; it wrecked her entire life. Because her mother was no longer alive, Jalil married her to Rasheed. She realized fate and society were conspiring to destroy her. Acceptance of the Burqa is the first stage towards her domestication and victimization of Rasheed's culture. As all the shutters to the outer world were closed for her, all the horrible secrets of her history, she symbolically lost her view of life. Her multiple miscarriages are the main reason of her depression. She falls pregnant several times, but each time she miscarries, much to Rasheed's dismay. She condemns both herself and Nature for denying her the delights of motherhood. She gets ill and depressed, and she loses interest in life and its activities. Her guilt is haunting her, and she is torn in body and spirit. She is compelled to reflect about her distress. Mariam had been oppressed and marginalized in every way possible. She was emotionally, physically, and psychologically abused.To emphasize the horrible violence, Hosseini uses the animal imagery of a grizzly bear. Physical appearance of Rasheed is that of an ugly bear, with a large physique and coarse hair. Even though he states that: "Half the women in this city would kill to have a husband like me" (276). Rasheed has four wives and likes the sadistic delights of tormenting them all like a savage tribal warlord.

Laila and Tariq are sincere loves who intended to marry but were separated due to a change in government. Laila becomes pregnant, but Tariq must flee Kabul for his own safety. He was severely injured by a land mine explosion, but he never lost his bravery. Laila's parents are also slain in the fight. Rasheed takes advantage of the situation by informing Laila that Tariq has been slain. His parents had told her fascinating anecdotes about their romance and marriage. Her father had told her that she would like being married. Laila lived in a dream world because she had a romantic outlook on love and marriage. Rasheed married Laila because Mariam was unable to bear children and was barren. Rasheed is quite nice to Laila in the first year; he looks after her well and even gives her gifts. He repeats his habit of physically tormenting Laila after she becomes a mother.

Her pretension of being virgin indicates that even after going through a phase of extreme physical and emotional trauma and outrage, she has not gone neurotic, she shows the presence of mind, and tactfully handles the situation to survive in precarious conditions. Laila understands that an Afghan woman has to bleed well to prove her virginity to become acceptable as wife even to an old polygamous man. She does not take up cudgels against patriarchy; rather she undermines it indirectly and tactfully. She smashes the age old patriarchal belief of virginity. Laila shows that an Afghan woman can go to extremity when she and her baby are endangered. She becomes slyly submissive to patriarchy as she knows that survival against it is very bleak in a war-torn country. But her miseries do not end with a single trick; rather violence hits her viciously. Violence, savagery, humiliation and threats to her survival invade her life in the same manner as in Mariam's life. In a similar fashion violence permeates her life passively and insidiously. Rasheed repeats his decrees to his newly married wife;

"I am your husband now, and it falls on me to guard not only your honor but ours, yes, our Nang and Namoos. That is the husband's burden.

All I ask in return . . . Avoid leaving this house without my company. If I am away and you need something urgently, I mean absolutely need it and it cannot wait for me, then you can send Mariam . . . That you wear a burqa. For your own protection naturally. It is best. So many lewd men in this town now. Such vile intensions, so eager to dishonor even a married woman . . . Mariam will be my eyes and ears when I am away . . . But you are still a young woman . . . And young women can make unfortunate choices" (217-218).

Every word, every gesture and tone of Rasheed's utterances is full of threats and intimidation. He tries to evoke fear in Laila so that he may have complete dominance over her. He is insecure as there is always suspense in his mind of her escaping away. Laila finds her helpless and trapped in such desperate conditions. She pretends to be submissive but her strategy for survival occupies her mind. She abides by all commands and warnings only to bring her baby in the world. She always talks to her baby and doing this she creates her own world where she feels Tariq's presence. By her education, she knows how to hoodwink suffocating Afghan patriarchy. But she does not want to live in such an environment for long as she knows that this life is bereft of dignity and her soul will wither away. She has plans for better survival and she always works to fulfill them. She collects money secretly keeping in view contingent expenses. She does it in a way that nobody suspects her but a sense of fear of otherwise always seizes her, "She wondered what he would do if he knew that she was planning to run away next spring . . . She would pawn her wedding ring when the time drew close" (241).

Hosseini recounts Mariam's heroic conduct in the novel's final section, where she gets fed up with Rasheed's torturing behavior. Many of people were slaughtered, and thousands more were forced to flee their homes in search of safety and stability in other countries. Many changes had occurred in society, but Mariam had been oblivious to them due to her personal problems. Her life had become monotonous and uninteresting. Mariam had become a pawn in Rasheed's merciless game. She was only a servant in the home, always cooking, cleaning, and washing clothing. Rasheed enjoys thrashing her and abusing her. She had neither a wish nor a dream. She only lived to save Laila's and her children's lives. Mariam intervenes in order to save Laila. In the scuffle, she kills Rasheed. She is warned not to take blame for Rasheed's death, but she refuses and chooses a death sentence to a life of slavery. She is executed for killing Rasheed in her final years, but she is at peace with her. She has no sorrow for murdering the monster to save Laila's life. She'd made the decision to kill Rasheed on her own, following the call of her soul. Rasheed was a vicious beast, and killing him was a wise decision. She was departing the world because she had restored order to an otherwise chaotic situation. Her death was significant, because she was leaving behind a dear friend, a kind mother, and a capable guardian. Mariam has no remorse and believes she has performed a heroic deed by killing a deadly bear. She takes the risk of ending their exploitation and servitude.It is a cardinal sin in Islam for a woman to kill a man, and it is worse if the guy is her spouse. The Taliban order Mariam's public execution, and she is executed in broad daylight. Laila and

Tariq are helpless. They, together with Aziza and Zalmai, flee to Pakistan.

They begin to rebuild their lives, and after the Taliban is destroyed, they return to Afghanistan, repair the orphanage, and name their newborn daughter Mariam in honor of the woman who saved them. Although there are few instances of hope throughout the narrative, they do exist. The first such occasion occurs when Mariam, as a small child, has a question for her Mullah. She is unsure whether she will be able to attend school. Mariam has more hope than Laila, her adoptive sister whom she practically considers her daughter. She believes men like Tariq exist.When Tariq reappears in her life, she expects him to save her, and he does, but only with considerable assistance and sacrifice from Mariam.Though reality sometimes smashes the hopes of the novel's main protagonists, they never give up.The reader's optimism for the novel's characters is also a hope for the improvement of Afghanistan's conditions.

The novel's characters' expectations and disappointments are mirrored in Afghanistan's political vagaries, where each new ruler brings new hope, but those hopes are frequently dashed when the new ruler turns out to be even more of a sadist. Similarly, when the Taliban arrived and liberated Afghanistan from perpetual civil war and infighting, as well as the incessant shelling of Hekmatyar and his organization, many people cheered that the country would finally be free of chaos and disorder.

Some religious individuals thought it was even better that the country was now ruled by a religious institution, thinking that religion would bring peace and order to their lives. They had no idea that the Taliban's fundamentalist interpretation of Islam would lead to their deaths.The fact that hope does not change the oppressive situation. Afghanistan's women face numerous forms of oppression.They are subjugated by Afghanistan's rigid traditions, which deny them much freedom. Their men oppress them, taking advantage of women's powerlessness in their country. Most importantly, they are oppressed by religion, which is the root of all other oppressions. The story A Thousand Splendid Suns is about those oppressions.

A Thousand Splendid Suns is a lengthy novel with a complex premise. It is organized into four sections, each of which is further broken into fifty-one chapters. Despite the fact that Laila and Mariam have different personalities, Hosseini portrays them in such a way that they share the same fate in an authoritarian, violent, and male-dominated society. He depicts the story of Mariam and Laila, who come from profoundly different backgrounds but are tied by fate and share the archetypal difficulties and tribulations of being Afghan women. They fight for survival in Afghanistan, navigating the mud-strewn path of sexuality, hierarchy, relentless conflict, and heavy guilt for the faults of others.Womanhood in Afghanistan, according to Hosseini, is suffering beyond comprehension due to violence. Women are subjected to humiliation, indignity, oppression, and subordination, forcing them to create even the most primitive means of survival. When violence rips apart the social fabric, women are the most vulnerable and suffer the most consequences, losing all support and benefits. The wretched fate of female characters reveals how religious ideas and Islamic law practices hurt them and make them impotent. As violence affects them both directly and indirectly as a result of male hostility, frustration, and victimhood, their victimization becomes more intricate, sophisticated, and multifaceted.

Political instability, brutality, and widespread misery have characterized Afghanistan's recent past. The Afghan people's survival has been horrible and harrowing for three decades due to recurrent warfare. According to Dr. Vincent B. Netto:

"The sadand sordid tale of misery and oppression . . . A complex baggage of traumatic memoriesis the theme of Hosseini . . . Depict violence and death, resulting in a mass reshuffling ofpopulation and severing of age-old roots, resulting in dislocation, displacement anddisruption. More than honor it is an anguish that characterizes everyone's life. Violencethat is brutal and irrational becomes an abhorrent reality."

A Thousand Splendid Suns focuses on the double colonization of Afghan women, as well as the weaker elements of the Afghan social structure during these periods of warfare. The actions and conditions depicted by the novelist are realistic and faithful representations of several layers of violence and how people manage to survive in such dreadful and nightmare surroundings.When fundamentalists rule the roost and harsh conditions abound, women are the most vulnerable, according to Afghan history. In a country like Afghanistan, identifying and enforcing women's rights is tough.

Despite the dominant patriarchal culture in Afghanistan, and thus more restricted, oppressed conditions for women, Afghan women are not necessarily voiceless and powerless. Yet despite the dominant patriarchal culture in Afghanistan, and thus more restricted, oppressed conditions for women, Afghan women are not necessarily voiceless and powerless. These experts say that Afghan women have demonstrated their ability to fight, survive, and participate in social activities in order to reclaim their rights and advance their advancement. Women have endured unbearable agony during three decades of unrelenting brutality, but they have done so with extraordinary courage, fortitude, and endurance. Women have always established their own survival strategies. Women in Afghanistan have valiantly proved their potential to create means of coping with life even under the most extreme types of coercion. Women have lived through 22 years of war, civil war, and violent struggle as social agents, and have explored alternate ways to survive and formulate their goals in a framework of limited resources and restrictive cultural practices.

The women in A Thousand Splendid Suns are actual people, and their survival is the novel's most compelling motif. The novel is atale of suffering and atonement,yet the brutal reality of conflict in the country sounds throughout the work. External forces lead the characters to suffer. The novel tackles the same topics, but from a feminist perspective,women are victims of various sorts of domestic and external violence, while men are victims of external violence because of political considerations. Characters' violence, defences, and coping mechanisms are not simple and uniform; rather, they are interconnected, complex, convoluted and multilayered.

# CHAPTER FIVE

# CONCLUSION

Khaled Hosseini is a man with an organic intuition who is continually looking beyond the limitations of the average human being. His main concern is the survival of the oppressed and persecuted people of Afghanistan. He has not portrayed any of his protagonists as a terrorist, fundamentalist, political activist, contrary to popular belief. His main concern is always the survival of the oppressed ordinary Afghans who are persecuted, victimized and downtrodden. Unlike popular belief, He has not presented any of his heroes as terrorists, contrary to popular belief Taliban fundamentalist, or political activist. In his works, Hosseini clearly depicted Afghanistan's political situation. He was aware of the political upheaval in his nation, while not residing there and reflected it in his work. This contributed authenticity to his art since in "A Thousand Splendid Suns" and "The Kite Runner," he accurately depicted the era of Soviet invasion and Taliban control.

Hosseini asserts that the struggle of survival is not a uniform phenomenon in Afghanistan. It is different for different sects and genders. The condition of ethnicminorities who are blatantly discriminated against is very deplorable and miserable. The burden of maintaining social relations is always on the oppressed rather than the oppressor, which makes life more wretched for them.

The present study of Khaled Hosseini's two books The Kite Runner and A Thousand Splendid Suns set against the backdrop of Afghanistan's civil war and Taliban rule, aims to uncover the tale of a nation, Afghanistan. Persecuted from within and without, is the true protagonist. It also provides a new perspective, a perspective on contextualizing the Afghan people's concept of self-identity immigrant experiences, debunking myths and preconceptions about the Taliban, people of Afghanistan as well as breaking down cultural barriers. Despite the politically correct official party stance, rifts between different communities in Afghanistan have existed for a long time and continue to exist now. Ethnic disparities and problems between different groups, which continue to plague society and threaten to stymie its development toward a better tomorrow, are best addressed head on. If we fail to face the past and the disparities, we will never be able to move on and overcome them.

The Kite Runner, written in 2003, piqued readers' interest in the increasingly famous Islamic nation of Afghanistan, then drew them in with a truly touching and romantic melodrama of lifelong friendship, deceit, Taliban cruelty, and redemption. The narrative affirmed the humanity of ordinary Afghans while criticizing their former leaders' barbarism. The American people's wrath and lack of information about Islam and the Middle East burst and devastated a nation after September 11, 2001. Hosseini concentrates on Kabul in the decades leading up to the Soviet invasion and under the Taliban in his depiction of Afghanistan. Hosseini depicts not only the beauty and culture of his boyhood Afghanistan, but also its societal flaws, such as religious differences and ethnic prejudice. Hosseini's Afghanistan is far from pleasant. The novel's crisis is caused by intrinsic flaws in Afghanistan's socioeconomic structure and cultural prejudices.

With A Thousand Splendid Suns, readers will gain a better understanding of daily life in Afghanistan, the urban-rural tensions that exist and contribute to the era of violence and upheaval there, and the catastrophic nature of each wave of war on Afghanistan's people and culture. Hosseini's story of a complex father-son relationship, friendship, betrayal, and redemption in The Kite Runner is set within a broader and more balanced vision of a country. In A Thousand Splendid Suns, Hosseini paints a much more detailed picture of Afghanistan, delving deeper into the country's past. The tale is set in many cities over the course of thirty years of conflict. The novel is set in Kabul, as well as Herat, Baniiyan, and Mariam's small fictional town outside of Herat.Hosseini expands on the basics he gave the reader in The Kite Runner, weaving the history of Afghanistan's lengthy succession of warfare into his second novel's storyline.The reader obtains a history lesson with Laila and Tariq as Laila's father informs the two youngsters about their heritage through the role of Laila's school teacher-father.

Hosseini's central characters of the novels who represents the essence of ethnocentric and gender based Afghan culture, are real people who are heartbreakingly sensitive to their sufferings. Minorities around the world have long struggled for survival. The male author was able to represent the story of women's concerns with sensitivity. It ultimately, the Hazaras and women pay the price, whatever else may be the case. The actual problems' foundation Hosseini has used the concept of double marginalization to his advantage infused personality, and rendered it in a fairly awe-inspiring manner. The Taliban, Pashtuns, and Mujahedeen, who wield power, are guiding the nation-state for their own profit, resulting in a pitiful situation for Hazaras, women, and children. For minorities who have only fought for survival throughout their lives, thinking about improving their circumstances is a pipe dream. Both of Hosseini's best-selling novels explore the effects of apartheid and its associated relics on the marginalized. This project contends that racist and ethnic foregrounds are just socially manufactured and are ingrained in each human since birth, causing them to condemn themselves and others, resulting in somatic incapacitation. Men-women, top dogs-underdogs, powerholders-minorities, wealthy-needy, and so on are all examples of biological aggression. It can be eliminated at all three levels of structural, cultural, and direct violence by removing the structural foundation. Physical, psychological, and sexual violence are more likely to be managed if structural-ideological violence is addressed. In their early stages, rigid and hierarchical structured civilizations might encourage egalitarian ideas by rejecting feudalism. Inequality, stratification, and ethnic imbalance are societal constructs, as is the Taliban and mujahideen concept of misunderstanding of holy texts through indoctrination, brainwashing, and coercion.

Pashtun community represents the major ethnic group followed by Tajiks, while others are minorities. These minorities have always been discriminated against by the dominant communities in Afghanistan. The minorities have always been ruthlessly subjugated and persecuted. Chiefly, Hazaras have always been at the receiving end due to the atrocious attitude of the Pashtuns. One of the first signs of the hold of religious theocracy is the hatred ofthe Shia Hazaras by the majority Sunni mullahs of the country. Thishatred comes out in almost racial terms, reminding one of the times ofSecond World War, in which Palestinian Grand Mufti collaborated withthe racial ethnical cleansing agenda of Hitler and killed many ethnicminorities in his own country.

In Afghanistan from the early period onwards interpersonal violence, ethnic prejudice, and violence against women and children have existed. In terms of women's roles in society, the Afghan social structure is exceedingly conservative and narrow-minded, and any attempt by women to assert themselves and break free from the limits of family life has always been met with harsh resistance and violence.The women of Afghanistan are oppressed many times over. They areoppressed by the orthodox traditions of Afghanistan which does not letthem much freedom. They are oppressed by their men, who take benefitof the helplessness of women in their country. But most of all, they are oppressed by religion, which is the primary reason of all otheroppressions.

Indoctrination is mainly responsible for the plight and predicament of a victim ofdiscrimination. Minority people fail to break out of the shackles, unleashing oppression,making their life embittered and dehumanized. Their struggle against the ordeals of life isfrustrating and very grim. To conclude we can say that in Khaled Hosseini's novels about the national condition of Afghanistan, about ethnic groups, about the connection between terrorism and Afghanistan as a nation has been presented veryobjectively. And the oppression faced by women. To secure those marginalized people's life is possible only through a secular administration came on power. The orthodox culture of Afghanistan change only through a long process. The illiteracy of Afghan society paves a major contribution to the social asylum. The only hope for the equality in Afghan society is on the hands of coming generations.

# References


**PRIMARY SOURCE**

Hosseini, Khaled. *The Kite Runner*. New York: Riverhead Trade, 2004

Hosseini, Khaled. *A Thousand Splendid Suns*. New York: Riverhead Trade, 2008.

**SECONDARY SOURCE**

*Afghanistan family* (2006), CIA; book of world facts, [Online: web], Accessed 8 August 2007, URL: http.www.photius.com/ countries/Afghanistan_society_family.Hmt.

Afhiyatulloh. "The Language Style of *A Thousand Splendid Suns* by Khaled Hosseini." Thesis. Cirebon: Syekh Nurjati State Institute for Islamic Studies, 2011. Web. 24 Feb. 2016.

Anderson, Ewan W., and Nancy Hatch Dupree. *The Cultural Basis of Afghan Nationalism*. London/New York: Pinter Publishers, 1990. Print.

Arshi, Asma. "Countering Marginality in Khaled Hosseini's *A Thousand Splendid Suns*." *Golden Research Thoughts* 4.1 (2014): 1-2. Web. 21 Dec. 2015.

Barfield, Thomas. *Afghanistan: A Cultural and Political History*. Princeton: Princeton U.P. 2010.

Barth, Kelly. *The Rise and Fall of the Taliban*. San Diego: Greenhaven Press, 2005. Print.

Bayly, Susan. *Asian Voices in a Postcolonial Age*. N. Delhi: Cambridge UP, 2007. Print.

Bhat, N.J. "Sin and Redemption in Khaled Hosseini's *The Kite Runner*." *The Criterion: An International Journal in English* 6.2 (2015): 283-286. Web. 16 Nov. 2016.

Centlivres-Demont, Micheline. "Afghan Women in Peace, War, and Exile." *The Politics of Social Transformations in Afghanistan, Iran, and Pakistan*. Ed. Weiner Myron and Ali Banuazizi. New York: Syracuse UP, 1994. Print

Chaudhary, Antara. "From Margins to the Centre: A Study of the Subaltern in Khaled Hosseini's *A Thousand Splendid Suns.*" *Research Journal of English Language and Literature* 1.4 (2013): 212-216. Web. 17 June 2015.

Chahal, Dhoop Singh, and Randeep Rana. "Marginalizing Hazaras:A Study of Khaled Hosseini's *The Kite Runner.*" *The Criterion* 6.3 (2015): 302-309. Print

Corbet, Bob. Rev. of *The Kite Runner,* by Khaled Hosseini. New York: Riverhead Books. 14 May. 2006. Web. 23 Mar. 2015.

Dar, Ab. Majeed. "A Feministic Perspective in *A Thousand Splendid Suns.*" *The Dawn Journal* 2.2 (2013): 650-660. Web. 17 Dec. 2014.

Djiono, Yulia. "An Analysis of Gender Discrimination towards Mariam and Laila in *A Thousand Splendid Suns* by Khaled Hosseini." Thesis. Jakarta: Bina Nusantara University, 2009. Web. 16 Apr. 2016.

Edwards, Jannett. " Expatriate Literature and the Problem of Contested Representation: The Case of Khaled Hosseini's *The Kite Runner.*" Research Gate. 12 Dec. 2013. Web. 8 Mar. 2014.

Farlina, Nina. "The Issue of Cultural Identity in Khaled Hosseini's *The Kite Runner.*" Thesis. State Islamic University of Jakarta, 2008. Web. 7 June 2014.

Fowkes, Ben. *Ethnicity and Ethnic Conflicts in the Post-Communist World.* New York: Palgrave, 2002. Print.

Goodson, Larry P. (2001), "Perverting Islam: Taliban Social Policy toward Women",

Bloom, Harold, ed. *Bloom's Guides: Khaled Hosseini's The Kite Runner.* New York: Chelsea House Publishers, 2009.

Hanif, Safar A. Rev. of *The Kite Runner,* by Khaled Hosseini. *ASCFo.* 4 Dec. 2005. Web. 27 June 2015

Hayes, Judi Slayden. *In Search of The Kite Runner.* Atlanta: Chalice Press, 2007.

Herbert, Marilyn. *Bookclub-In-A-Box: Discusses the Novel The Kite Runner by Khaled Hosseini.* Toronto: Bookclub-In-A-Box, 2006..

Malang: Maulana Malik Ibrahim State Islamic University of Malang, 2009. Web. 15 Dec. 2013

Hopkins, B. D. 2008. *The Making of Modern Afghanistan.* London: Palgrave Macmillan, 2008.

Hosseini, Klialed. Khaled Hosseini Official Web Site. Web. 29-jun 201 lhttp://khaledhosseini.com

Kazemiyan, Azam. "*A Thousand Splendid Suns.* Rhetorical Vision of Afghan Women." Thesis. University of Ottawa, Ottawa. 2012. Web. 19 Dec. 2015. Maley, William, ed. *Afghanistan and the Taliban: The Rebirth of Fundamentalism?.* New Delhi: Penguin Books, 2001. Print..

Malik, M.A., Murtaza, Ghulam and Shah, Kazim. "Representation of Power Relationships in *The Kite Runner.*" *US-China Foreign Lanquage* 12.1 (2014): 17- 26. Web. 8 Feb. 2016

Malikyar, Helena (2000), "Development of Family Law in Afghanistan: the roles of the Hanafi Madhavad, Customary practice and power Politics", *Central Asian survey,* 16 (3), pp. 389-399

Marciniak, Jennifer. "*Suns*and Daughters: The Role of Marxism and Women in Khaled Hosseini's *A Thousand Splendid Suns*'". *Academia.edu.* Web. 23 July 2011.

Miller, Matthew Thomas. "The Kite Runner' Critiqued: New Orientalism Goes to the Big Screen."Common Dreams. N.p., 5 Jan. 2008. Web. 18 Feb. 2011.

O'Rourke, Meghan. "*The Kite Runner: Do I really have to read it?*" Slate, July 25, 2005.

Sherman, Sue. *Cambridge Wizard Student Guide: The Kite Runner.* New York: Cambridge University Press, 2006